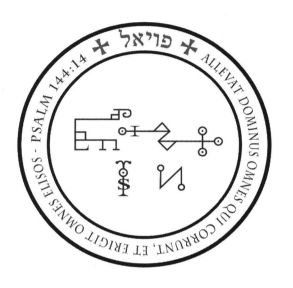

THE INSTITUTE FOR HERMETIC STUDIES
MONOGRAPH SERIES # 2

THE
THEORY
&
PRACTICE
OF
ENOCHIAN MAGIC

∞

MARK STAVISH, M.A.
IHS FOUNDER & DIRECTOR OF STUDIES

WITH

ALFRED DESTEFANO III
SERIES EDITOR

The Theory & Practice of Enochian Magic

The Institute for Hermetic Studies
Monograph Series #2

Copyright © 2016 Mark Stavish

Email: info@hermeticinstitute.org
Website: www.hermeticinstitute.org

INSTITUTE

FOR

HERMETIC STUDIES

MONOGRAPH SERIES

The Institute for Hermetic Studies provides high quality, in-depth monographs for both the academic and practical study of Western esotericism. Designed to be of value to both the professional researcher and practicing student, IHS Monographs contain detailed references, annotations, and listings of source material for further research by the reader. Monographs which were originally issued in PDF as Special Reports by the Institute for Hermetic Studies have been revised and updated.

TITLES IN THE SERIES

Introduction to Hermeticism – Its Theory and Practice

PUBLISHER'S NOTE

This monograph is an updated and revised edition of our previous "Special Report – How to Study Enochian Magic," first published by the Institute for Hermetic Studies in 2004. Upon the Report's release, Lon Milo DuQuette requested it for use with his Enochian study group, to which we agreed. In 2008 DuQuette published *Enochian Vision Magick: An Introduction and Practical Guide to the Magick of Dr. John Dee and Edward Kelley,* wherein he states, "...in 2003 my O.T.O. Brother and Enochian magick adept Christos Pir sent me a computer disk of material from a marvelous Enochian seminar he presented in Pittston, Pennsylvania... . I assure you, I could not have written this book without these materials and the profound insights of this great modern magician." As noted in a 2008 review of *Enochian Vision Magick,* the Institute for Hermetic Studies sponsored that seminar by Christos Pir, for which we are grateful, and are glad to have played a small part in the continuation of the study and practice of this unique form of spiritual exploration and realization.

I will reign over you, saith the God of Justice. O Lexarph, Comanan, Tabitom. Move, therefore, and show yourselves forth and appear; declare unto us the mysteries of your Creation, the Balance of Righteousness and Truth.

— The Book of the Concourse of the Forces

Monograph Overview

- The Role of Enochian in Modern Magic

- The Watchtowers and the Æthyrs: A Progressive Study Approach

- Which Rituals? Is This What Dee and Kelley Did?

Introduction

There are few students of contemporary esotericism that are not at least superficially familiar with Enochian magic and its role in the lives of Dr. John Dee, Edward Kelley, MacGregor Mathers, and Aleister Crowley. Yet, despite the hundreds of printed and electronic volumes available on Enochian magic, many students still seem to have problems with the system. This has given rise to the belief that Enochian magic is inherently dangerous and should be avoided until sufficient "development" is made. Others have declared it demonic and state that it should be avoided altogether. This monograph will examine these claims, as well as suggest practical and meaningful ways of *progressively* studying Enochian magic so that it can become a meaningful aid in one's spiritual growth. This monograph does not repeat what is said in other works, but seeks to expound upon their ideas and synthesize them with various viewpoints, thereby making them easier to understand and use. Several specific works for practicing Enochian magic are mentioned throughout, and should be referenced if available.

The Role of Enochian in Modern Magic

In discussing the development of Enochian magic over the last century or so, at least two things can be agreed upon: (1) methods of using Enochian in magical operations are as diverse as its practitioners; and (2) there is only the broadest general agreement on when the study of Enochian should begin. We see Enochian magic as an operative system moving from its original home in the Second Order of the RR et AC of the Hermetic Order of the Golden Dawn, into French Martinism, tincting the edges of Wicca, and being re-written to meet the needs of Anton LaVey's Church of Satan and its offshoot, the Temple of Set. Of the modern practitioners, several stand out: MacGregor Mathers, Israel Regardie, and Aleister Crowley. More recently, Lon Milo DuQuette, David Hulse, Pat Zalewski, Jean Dubuis, Christopher Feldman (a.k.a. "Christos Pir"), Ben Rowe, and others have written of their experiences with Enochian for more private audiences or exclusively via the Internet.

Regarding the first point, there are three common approaches. The first is that Enochian is essentially "evil" or in some manner dangerous, and that it should not be studied. This is the position of Paul Foster Case, founder the *Builders of the Adytum* (B.O.T.A.). Case was a member of Thoth-Hermes Temple of the *Rosicrucian Order of the Alpha and Omega* in New York City, circa 1920. The Alpha and Omega was run by Moina Mathers, the wife and widow of MacGregor Mathers; as such, it was directly connected to the original Golden Dawn approach to Enochian studies. Apparently, Case had two close friends who practiced Enochian and went insane. Case blamed their mental health issues on Enochian magic.

A more modern authority, Lon Milo DuQuette, derived his experience from the writings of Aleister Crowley, as well as having a personal relationship with two of Crowley's associates: Israel Regardie, Crowley's former secretary and well-known occult authority, and Grady McMurtry, head of the *Ordo Templi Orientis* (OTO). The OTO was reformulated by Crowley and became, along with the Gnostic Church, a chief ritualistic vehicle for promoting and expanding upon Crowley's teachings. Crowley is central to the study of Enochian as a practical and workable system of magic, and it is his writings that are constantly used as source materials, often taking primacy over the original materials of Dr. Dee and Kelley.

DuQuette (well known for his life-long involvement with the OTO), in a work he co-authored with Christopher S. Hyatt, Ph.D., writes:

> I have found the Enochian system to be the safest, cleanest and most logical system of practical magick one can perform. But it is an art and as such requires

not only study and practice but also inspiration and
the love-hate relationship all artists have with their
craft.[1]

In light of Case's statements, the above is clearly a polar
opposite position. Somewhere in the middle we find Israel
Regardie's views.

Perhaps a word or two of caution might be added.
Undoubtedly prudence is required in this matter (the
study of Enochian). It is a very powerful system,
and if used carelessly and indiscriminately will bring
about disaster and spiritual disintegration. The
warnings given in connection with the Invocations
are not to be regarded as conventions or as plati-
tudinous moralizings. They represent a knowledge
of true facts, and the student will do well to take
cognizance thereof. Let him study the theory first
of all, so that he has a thorough knowledge of the
construction of the squares and pyramids. This must
be so ingrained within his mind, that a glance at
the Tablets will automatically start an associative
current which will bring up without delay the attributions of any given letter or square which strikes
the eye. Only when this has been accomplished, dare
he venture to the actual usage of the Pyramids with
the God-forms, or the employment of the Invocations
in ceremonial.[2]

[1]Aleister Crowley, L. M. DuQuette, and C. S. Hyatt, *Enochian
World of Aleister Crowley: Enochian Sex Magic* (Tempe, AZ: New
Falcon Publications, 1991) 59.

[2]Israel Regardie, *The Golden Dawn* (St. Paul, MN: Llewellyn
Publications, 1986) 627.

Dolores Ashcroft-Nowicki has taken a similar stance, stating that Enochian must be approached carefully and with respect, and not over zealously, particularly by someone completely new to practical magic. During an interview[3] she stated:

> Enochian is very tonal. One of our supervisors left many years ago, in order to take up Enochian. He's a very, very competent occultist, a very good ritualist. Quite a down-to-earth person, and two years later he was a nervous wreck. He'd set aside one room in his house as a temple, furnished it, and for two years, almost every day had spent some time in there either practicing a call, or doing longer Enochian rituals. It started with him going in one day and finding all of the furniture piled in one end of the room. He put it back again, and said to himself, this did not happen. It happened again, and again, and finally one day he found his altar upside-down. He de-consecrated the entire place and shut it out. And said, "I can't do this anymore." Whatever "It" was thought well maybe he doesn't want to do it anymore, but "It" did. He began to find things around the house, all bundled in a corner, standing on top of one another. He came in one day and found two of his books, one flat, one on edge, and a glass of water standing on top. He tried everything, he blessed the house, cleansed the house, and called in a priest and had

---

[3]"An Interview with Dolores Ashcroft-Nowicki" by Mark Stavish. First published in *The Stone*, the Journal of The Philosophers of Nature (1996). Available at: www.hermeticinstitute.org.

it exorcised. One of the things people don't know
about exorcism is that you can't really use exorcism
on things that are older than Christianity. In the
end he gave up all forms of the occult, sold all of
his books, but not before he damn-near came to the
edge of a nervous breakdown.

When asked why Enochian magic was so hard-hitting,
Ashcroft-Nowicki replied:

It's sonics. Sound-vibration is the basis of the universe. All those little vortices may get sent going
the other way. Sound is really very powerful. We
haven't gotten quite to grips with that now. I know
for a fact that there are defense systems based on
sonics. I say I don't do any (Enochian), but I was
persuaded by Herbie Brennan, a couple of years ago,
at a Masters Class, to join in an Enochian ceremony,
which was for invisibility. This was a Saturday night,
my daughter was driving up from Yorkshire, the following morning. Now where we held this is in a place
called Wellington Park, and it is up on a hill. From
the top of the hill you can see six counties. Tammy
was driving up. We were saying isn't this a beautiful
day, you can see Worcester, and Silvershire, and Lin-
colnshire, and Tammy was going round and round,
because she couldn't find the place. When she finally
got there, two-and-a-half hours late. She said the
fog was incredible. We said what fog? She said,
"What have you two been doing, making yourselves
invisible?" She didn't even know we were doing this

particular ritual.[4]

Jean Dubuis, founder of the French alchemical-qabalistic organization *The Philosophers of Nature* (LPN)[5] authored a course on Enochian magic only to withdraw and destroy it. Some of his concerns regarding Enochian are presented herein. However, the most often cited is lack of preparation, and the desire to use Enochian for practical (mundane) purposes, before getting a feel for how the system works.

The second point, however, may solve some of the questions and safety issues that some of our authorities have stated. When is the best time to begin studying Enochian magic? Clearly, Regardie is of the opinion that extensive intellectual and theoretical understanding is critical and a prerequisite to actual ceremonial work. DuQuette, et al., does not state anything, but it can be inferred from their position that Enochian is "the safest system of magic they know of" and it could even be performed by someone with very little actual knowledge or experience in ritual magic.

---

[4]This ritual can be found in J. H. Brennan, *Magick for Beginners* (St. Paul, MN: Llewellyn Publications, 1998).

[5]"Les Philosophes du Nature" (LPN) was founded in France in 1979. It is no longer active, but its course materials on qabala, alchemy, spagyrics, and general esotericism can be obtained through various Internet sites.

Tools of the Trade

In order to study Enochian you will need:

1. Copies of the Elemental Tablets;
2. The Tablet of Union;
3. The 19 Calls;
4. The Thirty *Æthyrs*;
5. A copy of the *Sigillum Dei Æmeth* (see figure on page 25) is helpful but not required;
6. A notebook for recording your experiences and operations;
7. A notebook for writing out by hand the hierarchies, Calls, list of Æthyrs and their Governors, and related technical notes on pronunciation, ritual tools, and considerations, and anything directly concerned with the theoretical or technical aspects of the system.

Above are the bare-bones requirements. Some altar coverings can be used to match the Elements being used. A simple black cover is acceptable. If you work with the Golden Dawn or a similar system, your Elemental tools should be present and utilized when appropriate for their Element, but they are not essential.

It may sound like a great deal of work to write these things out by hand, but the Calls are short, the lists of hierarchies will be referred to often, and technical notes should be where you can read them when you need them. All of this will aid in impressing the ideas and angelic beings into your consciousness, thereby making your practices a little easier. If you are not willing to properly prepare yourself for using Enochian, then heed Israel Regardie's advice and *walk away*.

Even if it is, as some say, the "easiest and most friendly system" they have ever used, a certain degree of technical preparation is required.

Study Plan

Since the publishing of Crowley's *The Equinox* and Regardie's *The Golden Dawn*, the Lesser Banishing Ritual of the Pentagram and the Lesser Banishing Ritual of the Hexagram have become common stock in magical practices. For this reason, these rituals are not going to be described or discussed here, as any book on Enochian has them listed (and they are available on numerous websites). The question arises, however, what should you do if you don't like these rituals and would rather not use them? It appears that Dee and Kelley may never have actually used the material they were gathering; during their skrying sessions they also seemed to have ignored a great deal of the standard practices of the day. There is no record of magical circles or the normal means of protection, invoking, or banishing being employed. It very well may be possible to perform these operations in a relaxed and non-ritualistic environment. However, given the additional power clear associations between symbols can offer, it is suggested that these simple rituals be learned and utilized for this particular work.

1. Operation of the 14/18 Days
2. Meditation on the Tablet of Union
3. Enochian Cube of Space
4. Opening of the Tablet of Earth
5. Invoking of the Seniors

6. Invoking Subquarters of the Tablet of Earth
7. Invoking of the Calvary Cross as Sephiroth of the Tree of Life
8. Explore the Vast Array of Association of the Golden Dawn
9. The Æthyrs – A Journey Inward

Preliminary Invocation

According to Pat Zalewski, the following quotation from *The Book of the Concourse of the Forces* should be said prior to studying or practicing any Enochian material:

I will reign over you, saith the God of Justice. O Lexarph, Comanan, Tabitom. Move, therefore, and show yourselves forth and appear; declare unto us the mysteries of your Creation, the Balance of Righteousness and Truth.

The three names used in the preliminary invocation – Lexarph, Comanan, and Tabitom – are derived from the Tablet of Union, and can be found in the First Enochian Call (governing all works of Spirit). They are the Governors in Zax, the Tenth Æthyr. These names are related to the influences of Chesed on the Tree of Life (when overlapping Enochian with Qabala) and the unique influences of the Three Supernals, or the Holy Upper Trinity, as it impacts this sphere just before one crosses the Abyss.[6]

---

[6]Pat Zalewski, *Enochian Magic of the Golden Dawn* (St. Paul, MN: Llewellyn Publishing, 1994) 45.

At this point it is important not to ignore the subtle suggestions being stated here. (1) Like Qabalistic practices, Enochian requires an invocation of the highest as a preliminary before any additional work is done. (2) The forces invoked direct the energies towards the Pillar of Mercy, as well as the sphere of Chesed, an important point in suggesting the "incarnation of the Cosmic ideal" which is the purpose of this sphere.[7] (3) The relation of these names to a specific Æthyr demonstrates that the energies of the Æthyrs manifest through the Elemental Tablets in the same manner that the various spheres of the Tree of Life manifest through material creation (Malkuth).

Operation of the Days

This operation is described in detail in Geoffrey James's *The Enochian Magick of John Dee*, and in a slightly different version in Donald Tyson's *Enochian Magick for Beginners*.[8] The ritual consists of placing the Tablet of Union in the center of the altar and the four Elemental Tablets either next to it, each in their appropriate quarter, or on the walls of the oratory.[9] Then over a period of either 14 or 18 days (depending on how the first day's instructions are read), the major parts of the Enochian hierarchy are invoked and bound to serve the magician. This is a very important ritual

---

[7] For more information on the role of Chesed in spiritual development see: *Wisdom's Bliss: Developing Compassion in Western Esotericism* by Mark Stavish (IHS Monograph Series – forthcoming).

[8] Both are published by Llewellyn Publications, St. Paul, MN.

[9] An *oratory* is where spiritual practices are undertaken. The word is derived from the Latin word *ora*, or "speech," from where we get the Latin word for prayer; it is the personal temple of the hermeticist.

and often skipped by would-be practitioners. The benefit
is clear: in a period of two weeks or so, one will have had
at minimum a quick and orderly experience with the entire
system in its original context. It is also a very useful exercise
for experienced practitioners to undertake on an annual basis
to be sure that their use of the system is balanced in some
manner.

The directional orientation of the Elemental Tablets given
by Dee is different than that used later on in the Golden
Dawn and successor movements. However, this does not
matter: the system works either way. Simply to prove this
fact to yourself, it is advisable to perform the Operation using
Dee's orientations even if you use the Tablets constructed by
MacGregor Mathers for use in the Golden Dawn. Such an
experiment will demonstrate the flexibility of Enochian; it
will also function as a subtle form of "preventative medicine"
against developing a dogmatic approach to the system.

Meditation on the Tablet of Union

The Tablet of Union forms the core, the central piece, of
the Enochian universe, and is a synthesis of all the powers
represented by the Elemental Tablets. It can even be said
that the Elemental Tablets not only respond to the Tablet
of Union, they are an extension of it, and that without it,
they would not exist. Meditation on the Tablet of Union and
invoking its primary angel EHNB is something that is also
overlooked by many would-be Enochian magicians, much
to their deficit. Time spent with the Tablet of Union will
make future work with the Elemental Tablets easier and
more fruitful. One to three months is a good amount of time

to spend on this practice.

Enochian Cube of Space

Students of Qabala will be familiar with this concept as it is directly taken from the *Sepher Yetzirah,* where the Hebrew alphabet is used to construct a three-dimensional cube representational of space or the original astral matrix. In the Enochian Cube of Space, the ceiling and floor are created by visualizing the Tablet of Union for each and the remaining four walls by the Elemental Tablets. This is also another very important exercise that will allow students to become quickly familiar with the Enochian gateway they are creating and how to access it in a more pure "holographic" form. Anyone familiar with the Golden Dawn ritual "Supreme Convocation of the Watchtowers,"[10] which uses the first six Enochian Calls to open a ritual space, will recognize the value of this exercise. One to three months is a good amount of time to spend on this practice.

---

[10]"Supreme Convocation of the Watchtowers" is an expanded version of Israel Regardie's "Opening by Watchtower" and can be found in Chic and Sandra Tabatha Cicero, *Secrets of a Golden Dawn Temple* (St. Paul, MN: Llewellyn Publications, 1992) 312.

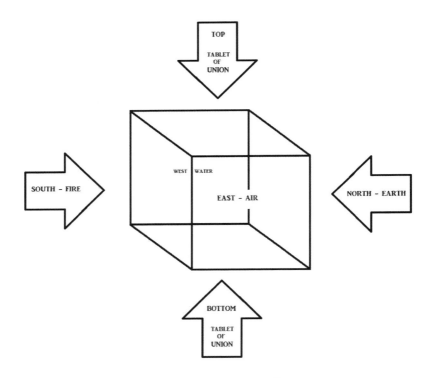

Enochian Cube of Space

Opening the Tablet of Earth

The work done with the Tablet of Earth represents a model to be followed with each of the additional Tablets in turn. When working with the other Tablets the order should be Earth-Water-Air-Fire (ordering in Alchemy and traditional Qabala), or Earth-Air-Water-Fire (Golden Dawn ordering).

Invoking the Seniors

The Seniors on the four Tablets in their most basic form represent the planetary energies as they are directed through the Elements, or individual Tablets. These energies are aligned very closely to our psychic centers, and in fact work through them in coordination with the Elemental energies. It can also be suggested that as these energies increase in density they actually form the Elements. The two work very closely together, but care is needed to not confuse which energies belong to which vibratory level of existence.

Traditionally, the Seniors are invoked using the hexagram. In addition to this, or if the hexagram rituals are not known, imagine the letters of the name flashing in the appropriate planetary color as the Senior's name is being vibrated. Despite its simplicity, this adds a great deal of activity to what is a relatively simple invocation.

Starting on Sunday, invoke the presence of the Elemental King, asking for its assistance in invoking the Seniors of the Tablet of Earth and gaining their assistance. On Monday, invoke the name corresponding to the Moon. Trace, or connect the letters, of the name with your wand, lotus wand, or Pantacle of Earth, imagining them light up in brilliant

violet or purple. Imagine that part of the Tablet of Earth
glowing in clear, bright, purple light. Then sit and meditate
repeating the Senior's name to yourself mentally to bring
its energy into your *"Sphere of Sensation."*[11] After a few
minutes, thank the Senior for its assistance, even if you were
not consciously aware of anything happening, and banish it.
Thank the Elemental King, and using the banishing forms
of the pentagram close down the Tablet. Wrap everything
and put it away.

Invoking the Subquarters of the Elemental Tablets

The subquarters of the Tablets represent the idea of a
microcosm within a macrocosm, or that within everything is
everything else in some form. While each Tablet is specific
to a single mode of expressing energy – Earth is solid, Water
is liquid, Air is gaseous, and Fire is dynamic energy – they
also have expressions of the other Elements intermingled.
From this we see Earth has a solid aspect (Earth of Earth),
as well as a fluidic (Water of Earth – Virgo), a vaporous
(Air of Earth – Taurus), and a dynamic part (Fire of Earth
– Capricorn). We often do not think of "Earth" moving, but
it certainly does in the case of volcanoes and earthquakes.
In qabala, these are the forces of Capricorn at work in the
material world. Nor do we generally think of it as having
a vaporous aspect, but we need only think of the breeze
blowing across rich, ripe fields and orchards to understand
how Taurus fulfills this description. The slow silent patience

---

[11]The Sphere of Sensation is the Golden Dawn term used to refer to
the aura.

of Virgo, paying attention to details and seeping into every crack and crevice nurtures the seeds growing silently below, just as the Hermit walks in silence and nurtures the inner light. From symbols such as this, we can easily see how the Tarot correspondences come into play, and make the various subsections of the Elemental Tablets richer in expression and practicality. To make these specific sub-classifications more concrete, the Golden Dawn gave each of the Subquarters to a Sign of the Zodiac. So, if you want to invoke the energy of Capricorn to move your professional career forward, use an invocation to the quarter of the Tablet of Earth relating to Fire: as we have shown, Capricorn is violent, dramatic energy in motion, and an Earth Sign. The Tarot card for Capricorn is the Devil, and meditation on its teachings and presence in a ritual will add to the vitality of the work undertaken.

Current Enochian magicians, however, are inclined to leave the Major Trumps for Qabalistic Pathworking, and instead assign the Minor Court Cards to the Subquarters, as well as the various squares on the Tablet of Union.[12] The Major Trump could still be present, however, representing its Astrological, Planetary, or Elemental qualities as they relate to the specifics of the ritual's desired outcome, leaving the more general energies to the Minor Court Cards. If you wish to leave the Tarot out completely, the Tattwas, an Indian system of the Elements using simple shapes and

---

[12]See: Lon Milo DuQuette, *Tarot of Ceremonial Magick* (York Beach, ME: Samuel Weiser, 1995). This book is very useful for its charts that quickly and easily allow one to know which cards and correspondences go with what parts of the Tablets, as well as the rituals to invoke those forces.

colors in multiple combination, are frequently applied and are a suitable substitute. It cannot be stated enough that Enochian magic is *fluid*, and that *systematic* experimentation will allow each operator to discover their preferred methods.

For those wishing to remember, understand, and utilize the various attributes given by the Golden Dawn to the Enochian components, a careful study of the Tablet of Union is indispensable, as each of the Elemental Tablets is simply a detailed extension of it.

Invoking of the Calvary Cross as Sephiroth of the Tree of Life

Each Subquarter has a cross surrounded by additional squares. This is known as the "Calvary Cross," and represents the influences of the spheres of the Tree of Life in and through that particular subsection of that particular Tablet. Each Cross is controlled by invoking two angels; in turn, these can direct those angels subordinate to it. In general, the Calvary Crosses, their ruling angels, and additional Lesser Angels and Demons are invoked in a similar manner. For the most part, it is not necessary to spend a great deal of time with the entities below the Calvary Cross, or at most the Kerubic Angels, as they are so very specific in nature as to appear almost inert to our consciousness. It is like talking to the street-sweeper when who you really need is the crew foreman or the head of the Department of Sanitation.

The Cacodemons

The Cacodemons should be avoided by all but the most experienced ceremonial magician, as there is considerable confusion and contradiction regarding their nature. They are described as being everything from unruly destructive entities to little more than mischievous Elementals. This is a very tricky area of work and should best be left up to you and your Holy Guardian Angel to decide how and when to approach it. In addition, it might be advisable to have some experience in *goetic* operations prior to working with the Cacodemons.

Explore the Vast Array of Associations of the Golden Dawn

It is important to practice Enochian in a simple form and build on one's personal experiences. It is clear that the system as revealed to Dee and Kelley was complex, yet different than what was produced by MacGregor Mathers and others. The most obvious difference is in the various attributions given to each square and their associated Egyptian godforms.

In the Dee-Kelley system, the letters are given for each square – and that's it. In the Golden Dawn, however, each square has its letter, as well as Elemental attributes. Since each square by definition has four sides, there are four possible Elements in each square, plus the letter in the center. For this reason the squares are often depicted as if one were looking down at a truncated pyramid, so that there are four sloping angles and the "top" or center square with the letter in the center. This "quartering" of each square around the

E	X	A	R	P
H	C	O	M	A
N	A	N	T	A
B	I	T	O	M

THE TABLET OF UNION

center allows it to be seen in precise ratios of energy relationships. When visualized three-dimensionally, the squares
are in fact imaged as truncated pyramids, but hollow, with
an Egyptian deity standing in the center, as if it were rising
out of the Enochian letter it stands upon.

The Tablet of Union is the best example of these forms of
energy ratios. If we look at it in the traditional Dee-Kelley
system, we have four words of five letters each forming
four rows and five columns. *Each row forms a word* – the
Enochian equivalent of the Element it invokes. The *first
column*, however, takes the first letter in each of these words
and unites it into a new word: EHNB. EHNB is the ruling
angel of the Tablet of Union.

When the Golden Dawn attributes are added, we find
that the first column not only spells EHNB but is also pre-
dominantly made up of "Spirit" energy. Each letter for each
square – EHNB – is three parts "Spirit" to one part Air
(E), Water (H), Earth (N), and Fire (B), respectively. Thus
each square is three-quarters spirit to one-quarter its natural
Element.

As the other squares are addressed, this ratio shifts to

fifty-percent Spirit to a twenty-five/twenty-five percent ratio, with the remaining two quarters each representing either a pure Elemental co-presence with Spirit or a mixing of the Elements. (See table on page 23.)

A simple examination of the chart will demonstrate the logic behind the mixing. Clearly those closest to Spirit are the Aces and the Hebrew letter Shin, as it is pure energy with the tincture of a pure Elemental differentiation. As we move across the row, each Element mixes with each of the other Elements in turn, as well as producing its own pure dense state of pre-matter, or a perfect balance of Spirit with just one Elemental vibration.

Example: $1/2$ Spirit and $1/2$ Air (X); $1/2$ Spirit and $1/2$ Water (O); $1/2$ Spirit and $1/2$ Earth (T); $1/2$ Spirit and $1/2$ Fire (M).

This Elemental attribution continues with the remaining squares of each Elemental Tablet, and assigns detailed planetary, zodiacal, and sephirothic attributions, (and through these, tarot cards as well).

The Æthyrs – A Journey Inward

Astral experiences of the Æthyrs are the simplest of all Enochian practices to undertake, and in many ways the most important. While the Elemental Tablets address the etheric and material energies of creation, it is the Æthyrs that represent the influences of the subtle spiritual energies that give rise to consciousness, that, in fact, *are* consciousness as we understand it. It is only by ascending the planes represented by the Æthyrs that we can expand our awareness in a way similar to what is done when "Rising on the Planes." While exploration of the Elemental Tablets will reveal a great deal, and manipulation of their energies can be useful or foolish depending on the maturity of the magician, it is Skrying the Æthyrs that gives us the experience of "Knowledge and Conversation" with our "Holy Guardian Angel." This experience must be the focal point of all esoteric operations if we are to grow as Beings, and not simply wander in an astral quagmire of self-created amusement or delusion.

Regardless of one's experience, working systematically through each Æthyr is important, as simply doing so stimulates some level of response, even if it is not as dramatic or profound as the magician might like. This is the same as working on the higher levels of the Tree of Life. Not everyone will have great insights as a result of working on the Holy Upper Trinity, but all will obtain the benefits of attempting to experience the pure Light of Unity. This aspect of Enochian is critical to the spiritual evolution of the operator and should take preference to other areas of work after the initial foundation has been built.

While Aleister Crowley's words on this topic may be a bit harsh, they stress the importance of this, and place all occult operations, regardless of their origin or tradition, in the proper context:

> The Magical Will is in its essence twofold, for it presupposes a beginning and an end; to Will to be a thing is to admit that you are not that thing. Hence to Will anything but the supreme thing [Knowledge and Conversation with one's Holy Guardian Angel], is to wander still further from it – **any Will but**

	Aces (Shin)	Princes (Vau)	Queens (Heh)	Princesses (Heh)	Knights (Yod)
Air (Swords)	3/4 Spirit 1/4 Air	1/2 Spirit 1/2 Air (X)	1/2 Spirit 1/4 Air 1/4 Water	1/2 Spirit 1/4 Earth 1/4 Air	1/2 Spirit 1/4 Fire 1/4 Air
Water (Cups)	3/4 Spirit 1/4 Water	1/2 Spirit 1/4 Air 1/4 Water	1/2 Spirit 1/2 Water (O)	1/2 Spirit 1/4 Earth 1/4 Water	1/2 Spirit 1/4 Fire 1/4 Water
Earth (Discs)	3/4 Spirit 1/4 Earth	1/2 Spirit 1/4 Air 1/4 Earth	1/2 Spirit 1/4 Water 1/4 Earth	1/2 Spirit 1/2 Earth (T)	1/2 Spirit 1/4 Fire 1/4 Earth
Fire (Wands)	3/4 Spirit 1/4 Fire	1/2 Spirit 1/4 Air 1/4 Fire	1/2 Spirit 1/4 Water 1/4 Fire	1/2 Spirit 1/4 Earth 1/4 Fire	1/2 Spirit 1/2 Fire (M)

G∴ D∴ Attribute Ratios

**that to give up the self to the Beloved is Black
Magic** [bold original]– yet this surrender is so simple
an act that to our complex minds it is the most
difficult of all acts; and hence training is necessary.

He further states:

The majority of people in this world are ataxic; they
cannot coordinate their mental muscles to make a
purposeful movement. They have no real Will, only
a set of wishes, many of which contradict others. The
victim wobbles from one to the other... Nothing
has been achieved, except the one thing of which the
victim is not conscious: the destruction of his own
character... How then is Will to be trained? All the
wishes, caprices, inclinations, tendencies, appetites,
must be detected, examined, judged by the standard
of whether they help or hinder the main purpose
[i.e., attaining Knowledge and Conversation with
one's Holy Guardian Angel], and treated accordingly.
Vigilance and courage are obviously required.[13]

Working with the Æthyrs is also a fairly accurate litmus
test of one's inner initiation. The Thirty Æthyrs and their
ninety-one Governors roughly approximate the spheres on
the Tree of Life and their guardians or gatekeepers. While
one can get a glimpse of areas beyond their level of initiation
(a fancy word for integration), they can't enter it. It is like
being able to ride an elevator to the top of a skyscraper
but not being allowed to get off when it stops, and only

---

[13] Aleister Crowley, *Magick* (York Beach, ME: Samuel Weiser, 2000)
62.

getting to peek as the doors open and close. On levels that we function at we can actually get off and walk around. The Governors as Guardians also act as guides in that they can give us the keys, clues, and outright information we need to proceed into the next Æthyr.

SIGILLUM DEI ÆMETH

Areas of Consideration

The following points are designed to stimulate individual research into the various contradictions that Enochian holds, and may help to arrive at some level of consensus about them.

Role of the Tablet of Union

The Tablet of Union may act as an amplification device, even affecting talismans or crystals placed upon it, by up to a factor of ten.[14] This is important, as a crystal ball is often placed on it for skrying purposes.

A Lunar System

Lavanah, the Hebrew word for Moon, is inscribed on the reverse of the *Sigillum Dei Æmeth*, and the majority of the invocations are aimed at practical and mundane affairs. Enochian, or at least the Elemental Tablets, may be limited to effecting Yetzirah, and in turn, Assiah.

The emphasis on sound rather than visual imagery, at least for the Dee material, suggests a strong Yetziratic influence.

> The five universes are often explained in terms of their parallels at the human level. Man's innermost will and volition correspond to the universe of *Adam Kadmon*. The level of preconceptual or undifferentiated mind corresponds to *Atzilut*. The process

---

[14]Zalewski, *Enochian Magic* 170.

of thought corresponds to the universe of *Beriyah*. Speech and communication parallel the universe of *Yetzirah* and, finally, action corresponds to *Asiyah*.[15]

Further on we also read:

> The term Yetzirah comes from the root *Yatzar*, meaning "to form." Yetzirah thus denotes the formation of something from a substance that already exists...something from something... . In general, thought is said to be on the level of Beriyah-Creation, since thought is "something from nothing." Speech, on the other hand, emanates from thought – "something from something" – and is therefore on the level of Yetzirah-Formation.[16]

Monday, therefore, would be the Enochian "Sabbath" or "Holy Day" of the week, and all initial Enochian practices should begin on a Monday to maximize this influence.

An Air System

Esoteric systems can be categorized according to their Elemental bias. Alchemy seeks to release energy, and thereby affect consciousness through working on matter, or Earth. Qabala seeks to affect consciousness through symbols that stimulate the emotions, thereby it falls under the category of Water. Astrology and forms of natural magic based upon astrological timing seek to capture and utilize the pure

---

[15] Aryeh Kaplan, *Inner Space* (Brooklyn, NY: Moznain Publishing Corp., 1990) 22.

[16] Ibid. 26.

energies of the solar system, and thereby affect consciousness in a pure and immaterial form, via nature's Fire. Systems like Enochian, that affect the fundamental organization's structure and relationship between things, is an Air system, and is approached mainly through sound, vocalization, and complex charts or hierarchies of relationships.

This explains a great deal, as the Element of Air is the cement that binds the invisible and visible universes together. It affects the brain, nervous system, and intellect. Yesod, or the Lunar influences in the Golden Dawn, are also attributed to Air, and the first Senior listed is a Lunar Senior.

Rituals of Air are the easiest to work with, as we can see with Enochian, but also the most dangerous in that a healthy balance of our Air Element is essential for life and consciousness. For this reason, you are encouraged to "Make Haste Slowly."

Thoth-Hermes, Lord of the Word

A close look at the Golden Dawn material demonstrates that in the higher grades of $5° = 6^{\square}$ and above, the lower grade material was the area of study. In the $1° = 10^{\square}$ or Zelator Degree, the candidate hears the *General Exordium*. This Exordium is a general invocation of Thoth, along with Assumption of the Godform, that is to be used in work of the Order. In fact, given Thoth's role in Egyptian cosmology and as the namesake of Hermeticism, it is to be done prior to all work, and particularly during evocations and the creation of talismans. Given that most of the material derived from the Golden Dawn, Enochian included, is taken out of its initiatic context, failure to include this alters the rituals considerably – a context that is particularly important if the student seeks to embark on a practical application of the complex Golden Dawn symbolism attached to the Enochian squares.[17]

> Above all the invocations, there is one that is fundamental – the Formula of the Enterer. This is the invocation of Thoth where the adept forges a magical link between him- or herself and the godform. Thoth is the link to our spirit consciousness and the adept must assume his form at the start of any [advanced] rituals, as dictated in the Exordium.

> By drawing upon the power of Thoth we can draw from a type of spiritual gene pool of everything that Thoth represents, that in turn gives us the power to command any entity invoked through him. Thoth gives us order in chaos, and he has the power of "accumulation" (for Thoth has recorded everything since the dawning of time) and it is that which we draw upon in our ritual. In psychological terms, Thoth becomes the archetypal doorway to Jung's concept of the "Collective Unconscious." Within the Golden Dawn his power is almost unlimited and transcends that of Osiris.[18]

---

[17]For more information on the role of Thoth-Hermes and practical use of the godform see: *Wisdom's Bliss: Developing Compassion in Western Esotericism* by Mark Stavish (IHS Monograph Series – forthcoming).

[18]Pat Zalewski, *Talismans & Evocations of the Golden Dawn* (Loughborough, Leicestershire: Thoth Publications, 2002) 198.

Enochian Supplies

The tools needed for Enochian can easily be made by anyone, and consist simply of black and white charts. However, the color combinations found on the Tablets is quite effective and many students suggest that they are easier to work with than black and white versions. Whatever the case, many soon find that making multi-colored Tablets by hand is a tedious and time-consuming task. Fortunately, large colored Elemental Tablets are available from several suppliers online. Smaller color plates of the Elemental Tablets and copies of the Sigillum Dei Æmeth are available through various Internet sources.[19] In addition, students will benefit from viewing *Enochian Magick: The Practice of Angelic Evocation,* a one-hour video on the history, theory, and practice of Enochian magic, complete with several ritual demonstrations.[20]

---

[19]Including Original Falcon Press; at the time of writing, they offer free, downloadable versions of all Tablets: http://www.originalfalcon.com/enochian_tablets.php.

[20]This video is by Lon Milo DuQuette, and produced by Hooded Man Productions, Claremont, CA (1994).

What to Expect – Journaling is Your Friend

A complete record of your Enochian experiments and practices is essential. Unlike other systems of magic, Enochian seems to take on a very personal bias, yet still retains characteristics that set it apart from other systems. This is reflected in the dream life of the operator.

If symbols are the key to our inner world, then dreams are our first steps on the porch of invisible temple. Themes will very quickly appear in your dream life, and repeat themselves in a manner not always seen in other systems. It is important that these themes be recognized, as they act as guides or clues to the next area of operation.

While it is not possible to say for sure what will happen, as Enochian seems to act more like a psychic steroid or vitamin rather than as an independent system, some general statements can be made about its effects. When used in conjunction with other systems, Enochian seems to add to their potency and impact; when used alone, as maybe it was intended when initially revealed, it stimulates each magician's own inner symbol set and personal mythology.

Here are some of the broad generalities that have taken place and unite the various experiences of Enochian researchers. These include, but are not limited to, the following:

1. Enochian entities often appear very thin, are striking in their contrasts of light and dark, and seem indifferent to human presence.
2. This indifference has even been described as "snob-

bery."

3. Dreams often involve motion and transportation.
4. Structures are often present such as buildings or streets, or more abstract types, involving squares, rectangles, and cubes.
5. Dream life is amplified considerably.
6. Right angles and directions are often encountered, possibly suggesting actual movement on the Tablet or sub-quadrant being worked with.
7. Verbal communication, often involving the Enochian language but not always, is encountered.
8. Erotic dreams are encountered or heightened.

Additional Forms of Enochian Magic

In addition to the Elemental Tablets and the Æthyrs, several other forms of Enochian magic were revealed to (or devised by) Dee and Kelley. These include, but are not limited to, working with the forces inscribed upon the Sigillum Dei Æmeth, opening the Twelve Gates, the planetary Angels of the Bonorum, or the *Heptarchia Mystica*, and the use of the *Tabula Sancta*, or Holy Table described in Dee's *Heptarchia Mystica*. Each of these areas of operation would constitute a paper or book in its own right. Students wishing to further pursue these studies should consult Pat Zalewski's *Golden Dawn Enochian Magic* and *John Dee's Five Books of Mystery: Original Sourcebook of Enochian Magic*, edited by Joseph H. Peterson, compiled from the collected works titled *Mysteriorum Libri Quinque*.

Conclusion

By now the average student should have grasped the fundamental idea that while it is possible to present information on Enochian magic for beginning students of the system, Enochian is not for beginners of magic. Dr. Dee was well advanced in his studies of theoretical and practical Hermeticism by the time he and Kelley began receiving the Enochian messages. MacGregor Mathers placed the material firmly in the Second Order practices of the Golden Dawn (or the "RR et AC"). Crowley was already firmly established as an exceptionally skilled ritualist when he began his romance with Enochian. Even modern authors who write on the subject in order to clarify and simplify the material for a new generation of ceremonialists have all had years of experience in Qabala, the Golden Dawn, or related forms of systematic instruction prior to their foray into the Elemental Tablets and the Æthyrs.

If individuals have problems with Enochian, it is most likely that Enochian is not the source of their angst, but rather their own ill-preparedness for operating it. All systems of magic function in and through the operator. If the individual's subconscious is relatively stable, their experiences will reflect this. If they come to magic, as many do, seeking a short-cut to solving life's problems without changing anything within themselves, this will be reflected in the pathological response of the system. As Regardie has hinted, too many students seek to find practical applications for Enochian, or magic in general, before they understand the theory. This lack of inner groundwork is a clear demonstration of a thinly veiled materialism covering their reasons for study.

Enochian, like all systems of esoteric study, is undertaken so that we can "become" more, rather than "have" more. If your goal is to grow in the Light, then you will have fewer issues. If your goal is to escape the problems of life and its material concerns, you will be damning yourself to potentially serious problems. As you become more whole and complete within yourself, more will be available to you in the world. Remember the axiom of Jesus, "Seek ye first the Kingdom of Heaven, and all things will be added unto you."

Enochian is an extremely fluid and adaptable system that responds to the intention and true inner desire of the operator in a manner that becomes extremely clear after even the slightest experience with it. In many ways it is comparable to a kind of high-octane fuel or high voltage energy source that is layered on to an existing system, such as the Golden Dawn has done. In this case, however, the vehicle and the driver are one in the person of the magician. If the vehicle is not stable enough to handle the increased power and available speed, it is their own fault and not that of the fuel they use.

It is easy to see why many people ask, "Why study Enochian magic at all?" Its apparent complexity and dubious reputation are enough to make one walk away. However, after reading the present monograph, it is hoped that each reader will be able to answer the above question enthusiastically, even with a hint of proselytizing in their voice as they point out the three main benefits of Enochian. As we have seen, (1) the system works simply and easily as a stand-alone method; (2) it adds considerable energy to whatever other system it is paired with; and finally (3) for those looking for a "grand synthesis" of Western magical techniques and symbols, Enochian offers a useful filing system that embraces the known ritualistic arts in a practical manner.

The rituals in their most basic form are little more than templates, or "Chinese menus," in which the same basic pattern is repeated with minor variations or additions. This kind of "cookbook" magic was often derided, but in contemporary society where time is precious and results needed, it offers substantial benefits over having to reinvent the wheel every time a ritual is performed. In addition, by repeating the same formula over and over, it embeds itself deeper and deeper into our subconscious, thereby creating a powerful and useful link that is unmatched. A careful reading of the examples given below, as well as in the various texts referred to, will demonstrate the sheer simplicity and adaptability of this peculiar and mysterious system of magic.

Summary

1. There are several conflicting views regarding Enochian magic. Despite this, it has been used by a variety of systems ranging from the Golden Dawn to the Temple of Set.

2. The Golden Dawn tradition states that Enochian is a very powerful system of magic and potentially dangerous, thereby requiring substantial preparation. Other modern practitioners are of the opinion that Enochian is not dangerous but instead quite user-friendly to novice magicians.

3. The fundamental power of Enochian comes from sound, and the pronunciation of the various calls in the Enochian language.

4. There are several schools of pronunciation, but none are in agreement. In the end, each magician must practice vibrating the sounds until they discover their own method of saying the words.

5. Enochian requires few tools and can be practiced with few or none of the standard magical devices.

6. Enochian can be practiced as a stand-alone system or as an adjunct to existing practices.

7. Enochian is deceptively simple, but still requires a solid and methodical plan of study to understand how it is arranged and, more importantly, how the magician will respond to the various operations.

8. Modern Enochian magicians focus their attention in two areas: the Elemental Tablets and the Æthyrs.

9. The Elemental Tablets have been revised several times by some modern authors (as they were originally, also, by Dee and Kelley).

10. The Elemental Tablets affect the material world as well as our inner "landscape." The Æthyrs are closer to the Qabalistic practice of "Rising on the Planes," and directly expand the magician's consciousness in a series of thirty distinct planes or levels.

11. It is important to balance out one's personal work between the Elemental Tablets and the Æthyrs. They interact with one another and assist in developing a balanced understanding of the system.

12. A notebook containing detailed information regarding one's experiments must be kept, particularly since the most immediate impact will be on the magician's dream life.

Appendix One
Simple Opening for the Tablet of Earth

1. Perform the Lesser Banishing Ritual of the Pentagram.
2. Perform the Lesser Banishing Ritual of the Hexagram.
3. Invoke the Three-Fold Name tracing the Grand Cross
   over the Tablet, vertical bar followed by horizontal bar.
   Imagine the letters flashing as you trace over them and
   recite the Names.
     (a) "In the Name and Power of the Three-Fold Name
          on the Banner of the North (trace line from top to
          bottom of tablet as you recite) Emor Dial Hectaga
          (trace line across the Names from left to right as
          you recite), I invoke the power of Earth through
          the presence of Iczodhecal (trace the invoking
          swirl as you vibrate the King's name)!"
4. Recite the Fifth Key.
5. Meditate on the nature of Earth using the name of the
   Elemental King as a focal point, reciting it slowly and
   vibrantly inwardly.
6. When done, stand, and give license to depart. "I now
   release any energies and beings bound by this ritual,
   that they may return to their sphere of habitation,
   and return quickly, reliably, and be friendly unto me
   when called. Go in peace." Trace the invoking swirl
   in reverse, sensing the presence of the King departing.
   Trace the lines of the Names in reverse, horizontal line
   of the Grand Cross first (right to left), followed by
   the vertical line (bottom to top), and sense the Tablet
   closing down.

7. Wrap the Tablet.
8. Perform additional banishing rituals if needed.

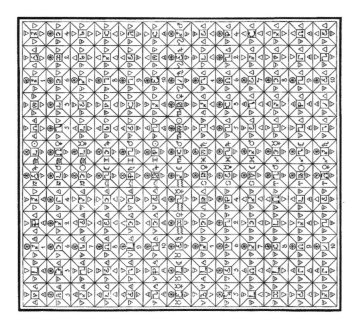

G ∴ D ∴ STYLE TABLET OF EARTH

Appendix Two
Standard Opening for the Tablet of Earth

Crowley's *Liber Chanock*, transcribed by Bill Heidrick and available online, is the main source for most modern Enochian material.[21]   The following ritual can be found in *Liber Chanock*, and is based upon the Golden Dawn Elemental Grade initiations. It is simple, clear, clean, to the point, and very effective. This invocation in particular is slightly longer than the ones for Spirit, Fire, Air, or Water, and for that reason is being given.

1. Perform Lesser Banishing Ritual of the Pentagram.
2. Perform Lesser Banishing Ritual of the Hexagram.
3. Purify with Fire and Water and announce, "The Temple is cleansed."
4. [Knock Once] "Let us adore the Lord and King of Earth!"
    (a) "Adonai ha-Aretz, Adonai Melekh, unto Thee be the Kingdom, the Sceptre, and the Splendour: Malkuth, Geburah, Gedulah, the Rose of Sharon and the Lily of the Valley, Amen!"
5. [Sprinkle Salt before the Tablet of Earth] "Let the Earth adore Adonai!"

---

[21]The text is also available in *Enochian Sex Magick* (see "Suggested Reading" under "Crowley"), which has little to do with sex magic or Tantra, and is a fine book for clearly and explicitly describing simple and effective Enochian operations. While it is simply an explanation and clarification of *Liber Chanock*, it is essential reading for beginning students.

6. Make the Invoking Hexagram of Saturn.
7. [Make the Invoking Pentagram of Spirit Passive] pronouncing these Names: "Ehieh, AGLA, Nanta."
8. [Make the Invoking Pentagram of Earth] pronouncing this Name: "Adonai Melekh!"
9. "And Elohim said: Let us make Man in Our own image; and let them have dominion over the Fish of the Sea and over the fowl of the Air: and over every creeping thing that creepeth upon the Earth. And the Elohim created Æth-Ha-Adam: in the image of the Elohim created They them; male and female created They them. In the Name of Adonai Melekh, and of the Bride and Queen of the Kingdom; Spirits of Earth adore your Creator!"
10. [Make the Sign of Taurus.] "In the Name of Auriel, Great Archangel of the Earth, Spirits of Earth, adore your Creator!"
11. [Make the Cross.] "In the Names and Letters of the great Northern Quadrangle, Spirits of Earth, adore your Creator!"
12. [Sprinkle water before the Tablet of Earth.] "In the three great secret Names of God, Emor, Dial, Hectaga, that are borne upon the Banners of the North, Spirits of Earth, adore your Creator!"
13. [Cense the Tablet of Earth.] "In the Name of Ic-Zod-Heh-Ca(l), Great King of the North, Spirits of Earth, adore your Creator!"
14. "In the Name of Adonai ha-Aretz, I declare that the Spirits of Earth have been duly invoked."
15. [Knock – 4444-333-22-1.]
16. Recite *The Fifth Key.*

The Keys should be recited in Enochian, although it is permissible to follow it with the English translation in order to become familiar with its meaning, as well as to evoke the required emotional atmosphere for the ritual.

The total time to perform the above ritual is about 15 minutes. It is then followed with a period of meditation, and a closing ritual. This may be a banishing of the Tablets, followed by the Banishing Rituals of the Hexagram or Pentagram. It is also common to do a simple banishing using the "License to Depart" and the Rose+Cross, and not repeat the banishing rituals a second time.

Appendix Three
Simple Invocation of a Senior

Perform all of the steps in either Appendix One or Two. After the recitation of The Fifth Key, recite the following invocation (Step 16). This invocation is used extensively and acts as a template for future invocations. All that is modified is the name of the angel being invoked and the selection of names being used by the magician for that purpose.

Enochian:

> OL VINU OD ZODAKAME, ILASA, GAHE [insert Name of Angel] OD ELANUSAHE VAORESAGI IAIDA, GOHUSA PUJO ILASA, DAREBESA! DO-O-I-APE _____ OD _____ OD _____ OD _____ OD _____ [use as many names as deemed essential]. OL VINU-TA OD ZODAMETA, ILAS, GAHE [insert name of Angel as used initially].

If you are not sure which Names to use, simply repeat the Names used in the initial invocation of the Element (Earth for example):

> DO-O-I-APE **Ehieh** OD **AGLA** OD **Nanta** OD **Adonai** OD **Auriel** OD **Emor Dial Hectaga** OD **Iczodhecal**. OL VINU-TA . . .

These Names do not have to be used, and other Names can be used in their place. There is no requirement that any Name or Names be used at all, as one could just as easily substitute "In the Name of my Holy Guardian Angel,"

simply making sure that the Senior, or Angel, being invoked
is named specifically in the appropriate places.

English Translation:

> I INVOKE AND MOVE THEE, O THOU, SPIRIT
> [Name of Angel], AND BEING EXALTED ABOVE
> YE IN THE POWERS OF THE MOST HIGH, I SAY
> UNTO THEE, OBEY! IN THE NAME OF _____
> AND _____ AND _____ AND _____ AND _____, I
> DO INVOKE AND BY INVOKING CONJURE THEE,
> O THOU, SPIRIT [Name of Angel].

Sit, meditate, and be receptive to what comes your way.
It is that simple.

Now, it is essential that the operator understands the
invocation being used, and that they create within themselves
the proper emotional resonance. Spend some time developing
a commanding, yet compassionate and just, sense within
yourself, so that when invoking the various angels through
this formula you may call them up from within yourself. This
is part of the basic formation of the "Magic Personality,"
and will go a long way towards ensuring the success of your
operations.

Appendix Four
Opening of a Sub-Quarter

When the angels of the Sub-Quarters are being addressed, it is important to pay attention to the hierarchy of Enochian. Invocations start at the top with the Three-Fold Name, followed by the King, but then ALL SIX Seniors are invoked, and two Divine Names from the Calvary Cross are used. Since there are several relationships of angels in the Sub-Quarters, additional angels can be invoked by adding their names. However, if you've taken the time to work with each of the Tablets, their Kings, and Seniors individually, the addition of the Calvary Crosses, Kerubic Angels, and any of the Lesser Angels will be easy to perform. It is simply a matter of tacking them on at the end in the order they belong.

Appendix Five
The Good Ministers of the 91 Æthyrs

One of the more interesting recent developments in Enochian magic is the exploration of the magical uses of the Good Ministers of the 91 Æthyrs. Traditionally, these "ministers" are understood to rule over various – although somewhat ambiguous – areas of the earth, as described in John Dee's *Liber Scientiæ*. It is believed that – given Dee's role as an intelligence agent in the service of Queen Elizabeth – it may have been thought possible to influence events in these areas magically. The adepts of the Golden Dawn appear to have ignored this terrestrial geography in their development of Enochian and its integration into their overall magical structure. Another magical group, the *Ordo Aurum Solis*, has, since its inception in 1897, worked extensively with Enochian, preferring a more simplified form over the more elaborate Golden Dawn style. In addition, the Aurum Solis appears to have developed a peculiar system of working with the Good Ministers of the 91 Æthyrs in a manner not previously done: for very specific magical operations of a mundane nature. The foundational premise of this work is that the use of the First Call is primarily spiritual in nature, while that of the Second Call is of a material or earthly nature. Thus, both poles of existence can be addressed.

The following information was sent to the Institute for Hermetic Studies well over a decade ago. It is believed to be from someone connected to a working lodge of the Ordo Aurum Solis. In addition to the descriptions given below, details on the understanding of the various Briatic and Yetziratic names were supplied, along with a ritual rubric.

All of this information can be found in *Mysteria Magica*, Volume Three of the Magical Philosophy Series by Melita Denning and Osborne Phillips (Llewellyn Publishing, 1986). It is being reproduced here because, despite their original success, copies of books from this three volume series and its five volume hardback predecessor can be difficult to locate.

The language in the ritual format supplied was consistent with that of the published material of the Aurum Solis. In our own experiments with this understanding of the Ministers and their possible functions, we took a very simple and direct approach – Calls were utilized, Names intoned, and Sigils drawn.[22] On occasion, we simply relied only on the power of the sound produced by the ritual itself. Notes from that time clearly state the occurrence of visions both spontaneously during the operations and later as lucid dreams. The quality of these visions and lucid dreams was unlike anything previously experienced. The color quality was a unique mix of light and dark, highly reflective, and not unlike that of color etchings or prints done on foil. The beings and landscapes were highly fantastic, and as one comment states, "Like something out of Tolkien's 'Lord of the Rings' novels."

---

[22][I.e., in the Aurum Solis instructions, the Second Key is intoned, followed by utterance of the Key of the Thirty Ayres (the "nineteenth" Angelic Key). The Name of the Ayre – or Æthyr – governing the division of the Earth associated with the chosen Minister(s) is used during recitation of the latter. Finally, the Name of the part of Earth is intoned (while inscribing its Sigil, if desired). – Ed.]

LIBER SCIENTIÆ
The Good Ministers of the Ayres
Ærial Subdivisions

1. **Rainbow-Vestured Guardians of the Limbeck of Blood (Water)**
Thy blood and thine, ye slain of earth, thy blood and thine, ye sufferers, is in the limbeck: yet behold, hour by hour it diminisheth, for the flame is set beneath and the spirit riseth up thence. Rejoice now with the keepers thereof! In all works of celebration shall they aid: in those also which seek understanding, courage and joy of spirit!

2. **The Dwellers in the Lake of Sapphires (Water)**
In perfect harmony and unity these inhabit, and in most sincere truth: wan are they and fair of form, and in their dark hair they twine as it were garlands of clear blue reeds. All that they may, they weave together: all works of integration will they make their care.

3. **The Flame-Clad Amethysts which Adorn the North (Water)**
Now like to the lightning, now like to misty rain are these as they dance: their music is as of cymbals ringing from a great distance. These will aid in rites to inspire followers for the Work, to charm away opposition, to win allies: but to win love to thine own self invoke them not.

4. **Lords of the Plain of Chrysoleth (Water)**
In feasting and gladness, in music and mirth are they

seen, who are all human of aspect. They hear and know strange and far things, and the thoughts of men. Of their dominion are works of consecration, and the making of the Magical link: also operations inaugurating new enterprises to influence others.

5. **The Angers of the Olive Mount, Captains of Ruin (Water)**
   These are seen as giants, vast of form and slow in movement. Yet do they swiftly hear when any calls their aid, if on three successive nights before that of his rite he will but take olive oil, mingle this with sand of the seashore, and macerate leaves of bindweed therewith: and this burning fumigate his place of working at the tenth hour of the night. Their aid is of high avail in works intended to preserve continuity in conditions of change, to perpetuate tradition, to mitigate the effects of vicissitude, and to promote loyalty.

6. **The Dwellers in the Pillared City (Water)**
   These have their abode upon a hill in shape as a cone and built from foot to summit upon a broad spiral terrace. Each round is the like of each, and each side differs from the others: so on foot move the Dwellers through variety, or move they by flight upward and downward in one aspect. Call thou upon these winged pilgrims if thy rite be for productive journeying, whether earthly or astral, or if the art of bi-location be thine aim.

7. **The Whispering Ones, Spirits of the Basalt Forest (Water)**

Forms of gleaming emerald, dwellers among dark boughs and shadowy leaves, they are but slightly hidden yet oft go unknown. Most bounteous are they, if thy works be of their kind: formation of an artificial elemental for benevolent purposes, or any other work to further the interests of other people.

8. **The Comfort of the Just, the Woes of Hyssop Rue and Wormwood (Water)**
These move in knots and in rings, armed with scourges: ever and anon they howl, as if they were smitten. Yet is their movement a dance, and their howling an oblation. These will assist in all operations intended to control the Lower Watcher or Dweller at the Threshold: likewise all works concerned with the fulfillment of natural responsibilities or with the furtherance of a mature attitude to life.

9. **Samite Robed Ministers of the Wave-Carven Altar (Water)**
These appear as maidens, with flowing hair and with eyes downcast: yet do they carry rods of power and commandment. They will aid in works performed to attain understanding of human needs, or in works dependent upon such an understanding: they will give assistance also in any work involving telepathy.

10. **The Lords Invincible, Leaders of the Silent Ones (Water)**
These appear as young women, vigorous and laughing of aspect. They will give assistance in all works of protection, likewise in operations relating to any aspect

of the upbringing of children: those to whose aid they
are called will be victors.

11. **The Mighty Spirits, Voices of the Throne (Water)**

Fast thou three days and call upon their aid in any
works of thaumaturgy, any works to be produced as
"signs" or "evidence."

12. **Lissome Ones of the Habitations of Twilight (Water)**

Their teeth and claws are marble white as milk, yet will
they offer no harm to the pensive or the solitary. If by
Art Magic thou dost strive to find congenial fellowship
or to gain from natural forces (as by gambling or by
agriculture) these are for thee. Yet, to keep their aid,
all that thou doest must be free from undue haste and
greed.

13. **The Panoplied Horsemen of the River of Dreams (Water)**

These have the aspect of young horsemen, armored as
knights, having over their armor surcoats of green and
gold. Pennons of gold with devices of green they bear
also upon their lances. The mists about the river part
at a shallow ford: the knights make the crossing in
joyous companies. The aid of these is to be invoked
in the high consecration of the Grail and in all works
of the Grail. Most potent and benign are they: yet
are the mists of that river filled with strange images,
and if thou dost undertake this work and make this
invocation, look guardedly that thou forsake it not for

aught else that may appear within thy fancy until this work be well concluded.

14. **Princes of the Waters of Death (Water)**
Changing winds and currents alike serve their advance. Call then upon their name for aid in operations to explore emotional experience, or to develop the imagination.

15. **The Governors of Continuance (Water)**
These blue-robed Ministers recline upon couches of alabaster and discourse upon the unity of past and future: for to them past and future are one, and are ever-present. They are to be called upon in works intended to nullify a force, or to affirm contentment and stillness, or for negation in any form.

16. **Guardians of the Wells of Pharphar (Fire)**
These watch over the unfailing sources of a torrent of swift radiance amidst dunes of crystalline fragments: they dip their hands to give drink of living flame to all who come to them. Works of fulfillment and of equilibrium are theirs: they are sought also in New Sowing, and for the transcending of time.

17. **Children of the Seven Thunders, Oracles of the Undefiled (Fire)**
Voices of the sword of lightning are these, terrible to hear: and for each voice shineth the face of a child of splendor, golden and ruddy. And these are the works that they will aid: to rule indirectly, to show the way, to teach, to heal, to nourish, to protect, to foster.

18. **Host of the Amber Ships, the Lamps of Awe (Fire)**

    Many and many are these, many and glorious. Their bodies are as flames of great stillness, and in each a most lofty and potent countenance. These will forward such works as to find entrance to other spheres: they are apt to aid such as would command wonders or would be instructed by oracles.

19. **Princes of the Salt of Wisdom (Fire)**

    Slight of form and placid of countenance, these are all golden in hue, golden is their vesture and very luminous are their eyes. Their aid should be sought in works of healing, whether of diseases or of injuries: also in works wrought to strengthen the Nephesh: also for rites inaugurating a new enterprise in a just cause.

20. **The Flame-Bearers, the Mighty Crowned Spirits (Fire)**

    Each sits enthroned beside each, at the circumference of a space proportional to the shadow of the Earth. Their countenances may not be seen because they shine so brightly: for each wears a crown having 64 points, and each point is a fire of radiance. Let thy voice go forth to them when thou wilt perform such mighty works as those which culminate in, or involve, resurrection or regeneration.

21. **Swift Ones of the Portals of Flame (Fire)**

    Deepest blackness is the visible aspect of these, but too rapidly do they move for the eye to dwell upon them. Theirs is the solution of specific problems: they will aid also in ceremonial methods of occult research, or in solemn dedication of thy studies.

22. **The Diamond-Helmed Lords of Vexation (Fire)**
Keen are their blades, a multitude: they guard the secret fords of Hakirath, and keep the last of the Seven Bridges, which is the drawbridge. Thou canst win their aid in works for sundering the magical link, likewise for works undertaken to achieve independence of environment or of associates.

23. **The Mighty Ones, Breastplates of Fire (Fire)**
As a great company of free warriors mounted upon wyverns, these go forward silently, one flame encompassing all. Their delight is in operations of transmutation: seek then their aid in such, or in operations for the realization of a paramount wish, or for the fulfillment of an ambition. To anyone of these will they assist: be certain therefore that it is thy true desire.

24. **Princes of the Torch-Lit Labyrinth (Fire)**
Mail-clad and helmed are these, and seated each before his banner: white and green, scarlet, azure and black tremble the sacred emblems. Ask thou the help of these in no work save one: the consecration of the spear.

25. **Iron-Shod Lords of Splendor (Fire)**
Horned helmets these bear, and cloaks of scarlet. The times of their full power are in the far past, and in the time yet to come: but in all ages are they awake to earthward. One word they heed from all who call upon them for aid: the name of friend. If they seem to defend

the bonds of blood and of marriage, it is but as the parties therein are also friend and friend: all duty they laugh to scorn, the self-seeker also do they laugh to tenfold scorn. Yet in works undertaken for friendship's sake, or for furtherance of a friend's interests, but call upon them and they will heed instantly: no offering they seek, and no promised veneration.

26. **The Governors of the Blackened Waters (Fire)**
These appear in form terrible, even as that which tradition averreth of sea-bishops: their bodies green and scaled, their wings, beards and the webs of their feet crimson, and having upon their heads seeming miters of violet and gold. If thou be so earnest to obtain somewhat that thou wilt have it at whatever cost, then before thy rite burn to them upon glowing charcoal a lock freshly cut from thy hair, with five drops of thine own blood drawn from thy right thumb, and sprinkled with some grains of salt of the sea: while this burns call upon these Governors, and state clearly thy desire.

27. **The Ministers of Glory, Summoners of the Harps of Iron (Fire)**
These keep their beacon-fires upon the highest summits: vast are the flames thereof. Seek their aid in works to influence public opinion, to propagate ideas and ideals.

28. **The Clarions of Orichalc, Ministers of Dissension**

29. **The Princes of Justice, Millstones of the Mighty**

30. **The Ministers of Guerdon, the Blue Flames of the Last**

31. **Tresses of Myrrh and of Asadulcis, Voices of Persuasion (Water)**

    Tall and supple are they, with limbs of youth, but their garments are heavy and dim as night and their faces are not seen. Some bear vessels of various shape, wrought of marble and of agate: some speak strange words of counsel. Their care is for works that would bring equilibrium out of unrest: also for works of transubstantiation, and for the art of talismanic consecration.

32. **The Noises of the Lower World, the Sighing Rumor of the Waters (Water)**

    Hardly are these to be seen, whether by sight earthly or spiritual: a sighing are they and a laughter, and a calling amid a wind: else are they like forms of glass that turn and move in endless swaying. Yet the heart of each is as it were a thin flame of changeful blue. Pour to them, before thy rite's beginning, a libation of white wine mingled with salt: upon barren earth pour it, or upon sand. They will aid in works of transformation, and in all works designated to produce change of circumstances.

33. **The Implacable Ministers, Living Lamps of the Concealed Shrine (Fire)**

    As heads graven of limestone seen in the midst of a

furnace, so fiercely and so brilliantly glow these in whiteness. Their assistance may be sought for works of levitation, teleportation, or any magical work with the object of transcending an obstacle or passing a barrier: only before calling their name, look thou dwell for seven days poorly, eat no cooked food, and speak no needless word.

34. **Wielders of the Blades of Division (Fire)**
These inhabit a fair garden, wherein the leaves and blossoms are of light. Their name should be called for aid in magical operations to explore philosophic concepts or to increase capacity therein.

35. **Dark Governors of the Powers of Pestilence (Fire)**
These are seen under the aspect of winged heads, their countenances expressive of most acute intelligence, their wings of lapis lazuli, gliding swiftly. They will aid thee for works performed during adverse tides, if there is need that such be done: also in operations seeking success in diplomacy.

36. **Princes of the Sanctuary, Rulers of the Forces of Conquest (Fire)**
All ruddy with sparkles of light are these, their faces and their vesture, as if they were of iron heated to redness. That which they try, they touch: if it be worthy it is transformed to brightness; if it be not worthy they leave upon it blackness as of burning. Theirs is the Red Work: theirs also are all works to attain renown and dominion.

37. **Keepers of the Mystery wherein are the Swords 600,000 of Length (Fire)**

Sandals they have of bronze, tunics of flashing crystal: in ranks and files are they seen, and each looks upon each with one countenance: also that which one of them does, they all do the like. The aid of these may be called for all works of Art Magic performed by means of a mirror, for all works dependent upon the powers of sex, and for all works effected to increase psychological perception or insight into matters touching the Astral World.

38. **Spirits of the Incensory of Confoundment (Fire)**

Wild are their whirlings and their hissings, these many-headed, these many-handed, with tearing fangs of steel and flinty claw. As scarlet and livid flames mingled with grey smoke they leap and writhe, and seek to draw all that they can within their clutches. Theirs are all works of malediction, of cursing and of destruction.

39. **The Daughters of Death, Guardians of the Secrets 8,987 (Fire)**

These go in majesty, with tall crowns upon their hair: winged are they, with pinions of changeful flame. Deep counsel is theirs: if thine be a work to attain the powers of interpretation, or to open a means of progress whether of the mind or in earthly things, or to find the keys of lost knowledge, these be for thee. Seek their aid too, if thy work be to prepare the Hand of Glory .

40. **Builders of the Wine-Press, Foundations of Zeal (Fire)**

Small are they of stature, mighty of limb, and their countenance is as the setting sun. Theirs is the pool of purple and the wall of hewn rock: huge works have they made, huge works shall make without speech thereof. To them commend works undertaken to gain leadership in social affairs, to defend a lawsuit or a matter of reputation.

41. **The Priestesses of Wrath, the Daughters of Storm (Fire)**
Swarthy are these of hue, jeweled with splendors: they move, they leap with potent flashings: they rend the vapors. Before thy rite, in a wild and secret place make offering to these of red wine mingled with honey, if thy purpose in working be to obtain good fortune in love, or toward the ceremonial making of a love charm. Do likewise for all works concerned with increase in personal attractiveness or in popularity.

42. **The Lords of the Column of Flame (Fire)**
Very powerful be these in high matters that touch upon the earth: in consecration of a new building or temple, or magical works undertaken to obtain such a building: or rites to purify a location of adverse spirits or influences. But if thou dost see the form in which these Lords appear, tell not of it lest confusion be multiplied.

43. **Veiled Sentinels of the Onyx Causeway (Air)**
As white smoke rising, beheld in a vertical and immobile shaft of light, so vibrant and so unmoving shine these. They celebrate established unity, even of the

highest: their power confirms the works of Unity Attained.

44. **Pale Queens Mighty in Sorrow, the Tears of Flame (Air)**

Their faces are of crystal, their robes are burning rubies, as with loud wailing they pass across a purple air. Before thy rite, call unto these in the dawn softly, and in some high place: so the work be to meet spiritual challenge, or to make assault upon enemies, to inspire them with terror, to rule them through their discords.

45. **The Mighty Sons, Reapers of the Harvest of Firedrakes (Air)**

Who would stir the forces of abundance: who is for honor, riches, health: seek ye these strong ones who exult with laughter, who gather and bind the terrible sheaves of destiny.

46. **Spirits of the 24th Part of a Moment: Timeless Movers (Air)**

These show themselves as men, or as lizards that go upright; but as figures seen across bare rocks in burning sunlight do they tremble and quiver, seeming for less space than a second to be gone. Thus instant by instant they go and return: and in the instant when they are gone, they are departed a vast distance to another place, even so to return. Thus do they almost dwell presently in two regions of the universe: thus test they knowledge by knowledge and truth by truth. Great is their aid for works of evocation, for works that require a very high degree of activity in the light, or of veracity.

47. **Calling Voices of the Bright Wilderness (Air)**
These are of a region of whiteness, which cloudlike builds to any form. They themselves appear most often in likeness of whirlwinds or waterspouts that sway and move with a gliding motion: but changeful and melodious is their song. They stir the minds and bodies of those who seek them with fitting rites, to the magical dance and to mystical drama in all its modes: any magical use of the creative arts is of their nature.

48. **The Smiling Brothers, the Sentinels of the Silver Castle (Air)**
In tunics of pearl, in surcoats of manifold hue, they guard walls of strong shining: their laughter is a lash of more avail than many arrows. Potent allies are they if thy work seeks converse with beings of the Higher Light, or if it be thy design to promote acuteness of intellect.

49. **Laughing Children of the Arrows of Cimah (Air)**
These appear as white mares rearing and plunging, casting from their shining flanks the purple and peacock breakers of a level shore. Seek their aid for all works of blessing, or for any works or rites undertaken in a spirit of devotion to tradition.

50. **The Princes of Power, Voices of Thunder (Air)**
Upon thrones of majesty these are established, each in his own hall: in heavy mantles of grey are they enwrapped, their hair and their beards are as black smoke curling upon itself. Their aid is given to those

who seek it for works pertaining to leadership in high projects, or to magical direction of human affairs: but they will not answer to the first entreaty nor yet to the second: utter then the Call of the Ayre three times for these Princes.

51. **The Garlanded Ones, Knowers of the Mind that Shall Be (Air)**
   These appear in the likeness of sphynges that have the faces of young boys, but old in wisdom: their garlands be of serpents, which speak to them, and to which they give drink of yellow wine in goblets of alabaster. These Garlanded Ones will aid in works performed to attain an understanding of living creatures, or in works dependent upon such an understanding: they will guide also in magical explorations of the realms of Nature.

52. **The Shields of the Sky, the Wings of Mail (Air)**
   Strong is the song of these, as the voices of trumpets or of the organ: at the sound of their coming, the columns of granite quail and lean one to another. Seek their aid if thou wouldst have any work that thou desirest performed by the hands of others: likewise for any work that is to be done in partnership.

53. **The Mercies of Everlastingness, the Vessels of Salt and of Honey (Air)**
   Pale Spirits are these, appearing in wide robes of whiteness: and in the midst of the brow of each, a shining flame. With them an odor as of myrrh, and of opoponax, and of lavender and of many sweet and bitter

herbs. Many of them bear flasks of tears, and jars with offerings to the Shadowed Ones, that all be done in due measure. Seek therefore their aid in celebration of all rites of the dead, whether funerary or commemorative, whether Samhuinn also or Parentalia.

54. **Empalled Regents of Splendor, Governors of the Glittering Fane (Air)**
These are seen as tall and stately forms swathed about in great mantles of azure, some lighter, some deeper in hue, some as the midnight. Their aid is meet for any operation that is performed to win ability to counsel wisely: if thou wilt call upon them for this work, on the eve of thy rite sleep thou upon a hilltop where is no human habitation, and on arising make obeisance to the place of sunrise.

55. **Keepers of the Mouths of the Winds (Air)**
The habitations of these are as craggy islands in a lake of silver. Their aid is sought in works for the development of practical wisdom, and in works generally of an austere nature or purpose.

56. **Shadow-Mantled Sages of the White Mountain beyond the Shores of Mist (Air)**
Wouldst thou travel in thy flesh or in spirit to the foot of the sheer cliff-face which underlies their abode? Wouldst thou win their esteem or compassion with rites, austerities, meditations a thousand times repeated? Nor weariness nor zeal will move them: yet if thou call upon their name, they shall assist in operations which seek to receive inspired thought or mystical

understanding, or to develop capacity for such.

57. Lords of the Heavens of Crystal (Air)

These are encompassed in a shining place ever-changing, with tints of the rainbow and with sounds of strange voices singing: very calm is their aspect. Their heed is for works seeking to explore and to comprehend music, natural rhythm, harmonies: also for all works dependent upon the occult use of color.

58. Princes of Dominion, the Mighty Princes of the Lesser Seal (Air)

Great is their power in all works which seek to produce reform: great is their power to release influences of change upon the earth.

59. Smiters of the Hands of Scorpions from the Necks of the Living (Air)

Pale are they, and their garments are as ashes: yet are their eyes of diamond and their hands as burnished blades. They fly swiftly without wings, and no place is sealed to them: they murmur, and the caverns beneath Barcaea have heard them. The White Work is theirs to aid, and also any work towards gaining new skill or power.

60. The Crimson-Robed Princes of the Wasteland (Air)

Upon the black rocks of the land of desolation have the Princes cast their mantles, and they brood wordless: arouse them not for light cause. Where works are performed for victory in thought and word, as in matters of law, they will aid: great power and high truth they will bring also to the consecration of a sword.

61. **Those who Pour upon the Earth Waters of Vision from Cups of Celadon (Air)**
Vast eyes are theirs, orbs of granite and of bland turquoise: some among them bear pallid cups of gracious form, others bear sweet-sounding harps. Grey is their vesture, girded with banded scarves of blue and russet and crimson. They will aid in works of skrying and of converse with Elementals: in all works which require services to be performed by true Elementals, these of the Waters of Vision if sought will aid thine authority.

62. **The Sickles that Chant of the Day of Reaping (Air)**
Their bodies are of silver mingled with gold, and in form as the leaves of tall reeds: greatly exulting is their song, but the words of it are concealed. They will give most strong assistance to works which would bring about the formulation of well-grounded plans, and the establishment thereof: also to works performed to gain visions of truth.

63. **Prophets of the Strong Tower, the Criers of Victory (Air)**
These will give aid in works concerned to establish or to maintain peace, inward or outward: also works to turn aside the weapons of an assailant or to avoid mischance.

64. **Daughters of the First, Strength of the Halls of**

Marble (Air)

These are seated at height and height: tremendous murmurings circle about them: in their hands are emblems of dominion. He who calls upon their aid shall gain it for rites of invisibility: likewise for works mathematical (such as the calculations of astrology) or other purposes of an abstract nature.

65. **The Comforters whose Eyes are Basilisks of Ruby (Water)**

Dark are their taloned heels, dark from time's wine-press and the vats of death. Turn thy gaze only upon their talons, for most dreadful is their countenance: look not upon it as in silence they come, but utter thy will if thy work be of their kind: mighty is their aid. These be for all works of Art Magic which depend for operation upon the material remains or the psyche of the dead (except such works as are comprised in 53 above).

66. **The Stewards of Fury, the Jasper-Headed Princes of Rage**

67. - 87. **The Powers of the Vials of Wrath**
(In operibus de sigillo ÆMETH.)

88. **The Hoarse Voices, the Thorn-clad Sisters of Vengeance (Water)**

These run barefoot over the land and upon the waters. With their hands they twist the spear and beneath their feet they trample the caltrop. They flee and smite not: yet through them is the slayer slain. They give aid for works undertaken to win success in commerce, for ceremonial works of divination in all forms, and for operations toward recovery of stolen property.

89. **The Beryl-Clad Ministers of Peace (Water)**
All veiled are these in a starry shining, bluish and greenish: and with them moves a shrill and joyous music of flutes. In troops do they go upward and downward, as moving in free air and not in bonds of earth. Works which concern them are those to further the interests of fraternal association, to give peace of mind, and for the circulation of earthly benefits.

90. **Bringers of Lights to the Feast (Water)**
These seem as a great host of small golden birds, but of countenance human: most rapid of flight, and their voice is as the chiming of bells. Before thy rite, pour unto them the water of a swift-flowing stream, if the purpose of the operation be to work a good of which thou shalt not be known as the author.

91. **Singers at the Hidden Loom in the Citadel of Truth (Water)**
These are mantled in sad colors and upon their heads are garlands of rue, yet do they go upon the backs of lions. They will assist if thou dost call upon them at the institution of the Great Work: also for works of compassion and for rites seeking protection during the night watches.

Appendix Six
The Elemental Tablets

The Tablets as given on the following pages are rendered using the characters of the extended English alphabet, following the *Clavicula Tabularum Enochi* of the British Museum's Sloane MS 307,[23] "likely to have been the original copy" of the Elemental Tablets, according to Skinner and Rankine.[24] They are presented here for ease of reference. (Again, for convenience, we have reprinted the Tablet of Union as given on page 20 of the present text below, though without any capitalization, as appears to be the case in the handwriting of Sloane MS 307.)

e	x	a	r	p
h	c	o	m	a
n	a	n	t	a
b	i	t	o	m

THE TABLET OF UNION

---

[23]Stephen Skinner and David Rankine, *Practical Angel Magic of Dr. John Dee's Enochian Tables* (Singapore: Golden Hoard Press, 2004) 58.

[24]Ibid. 39.

r	Z	i	l	a	f	A	U	t	i	p	a
a	r	d	z	a	i	d	p	a	L	a	m
c	Z	o	n	s	a	r	O	Y	a	u	b
T	o	i	T	t	X	o	p	a	c	o	C
S	i	g	a	s	o	m	r	b	Z	n	h
f	m	o	n	d	a	T	d	i	a	r	i
o	r	o	i	b	A	h	a	o	z	p	i
C	n	a	b	r	V	i	x	g	a	z	d
O	i	i	i	t	T	p	a	l	O	a	i
A	b	a	m	o	o	o	a	c	v	c	a
N	a	o	c	o	T	t	n	p	r	a	T
O	c	a	n	m	a	g	o	t	r	o	i
S	h	i	a	l	r	a	P	m	z	o	X

THE AIR TABLET

T	a	O	A	d	V	P	t	D	n	i	m
a	a	b	c	o	o	r	O	m	e	b	b
T	o	g	c	o	n	X	m	a	l	G	m
n	h	o	d	D	i	a	l	e	a	o	c
P	a	c	A	x	i	o	V	S	P	S	yl
S	a	a	i	x	a	a	r	v	r	o	i
m	p	h	a	r	s	l	g	a	I	O	l
m	a	m	g	l	o	i	n	L	i	r	x
o	l	a	a	D	a	g	a	T	a	P	a
p	a	L	c	o	i	d	X	P	a	c	n
n	d	a	z	n	X	i	V	a	a	s	a
l	i	d	p	o	n	s	d	a	S	P	i
X	r	i	i	h	t	a	r	n	d	I	l

THE WATER TABLET

b	o	a	Z	a	R	o	P	h	a	R	a
V	N	n	a	x	o	P	S	o	n	d	n
a	i	g	r	a	n	o	o	m	a	g	g
o	r	P	m	n	i	n	g	b	e	a	l
r	s	O	n	i	Z	i	r	l	e	m	u
i	Z	i	n	r	c	Z	i	a	M	h	l
m	o	r	d	i	a	l	h	C	t	G	a
Æ	o	c	a	n	c	h	i	a	s	o	m
A	r	b	i	Z	m	i	i	l	p	i	Z
O	p	a	n	a	l	a	m	s	m	a	L
d	O	l	o	P	i	n	i	a	n	b	a
r	x	p	a	O	c	s	i	Z	i	X	P
a	x	t	i	r	V	a	s	t	r	i	m

THE EARTH TABLET

d	o	n	p	a	T	d	a	n	V	a	a
O	l	o	a	G	e	o	o	b	a	v	i
o	p	a	m	n	o	O	G	m	d	n	m
a	p	l	s	T	e	d	e	c	a	o	p
s	c	m	i	o	o	n	A	m	l	o	X
v	a	r	s	G	d	L	b	r	i	a	P
o	i	p	t	e	a	a	P	d	o	C	e
P	s	v	a	c	n	r	Z	i	r	Z	a
S	i	o	d	a	o	i	n	r	z	f	m
d	a	l	t	T	d	n	a	d	i	r	e
d	i	x	o	m	o	n	s	i	o	S	P
O	o	D	P	Z	i	a	P	a	n	l	i
r	g	o	a	n	n	Q	A	C	r	a	r

THE FIRE TABLET

Suggested Reading

Asprem, Egil. *Arguing with Angels: Enochian Magic and Modern Occulture.* Albany, NY: SUNY Press, 2013.

Ayton, Wm. A. *The Life of John Dee Translated From the Latin by Dr. Thomas Smith.* London: Theosophical Publishing Society, 1908.

Crowley, Aleister, Lon Milo DuQuette, and Christopher S. Hyatt, Ph.D. *The Enochian World of Aleister Crowley: Enochian Sex Magick.* Tempe, AZ: New Falcon Publications, 1991.

Dee, John. *Diaries of John Dee.* Ed. Edward Fenton. United Kingdom: Day Books, 1998.

—. *Dr. John Dee's Spiritual Diaries (1583-1608): Being a Fully Revised and Edited Edition of A True & Faithful Relation of what passed for Many Yeers between Dr. John Dee...and Some Spirits...by Meric Casaubon.* Ed. Stephen Skinner. Singapore: Golden Hoard Press, 2011.

—. *John Dee's Five Books of Mystery.* Ed. Joseph H. Peterson. York Beach, ME: Weiser Books, 2003.

—. *Key to the Latin of Dr. John Dee's Spiritual Diaries (1583-1608).* Trans. Stephen Skinner. Singapore: Golden Hoard Press, 2012.

DuQuette, Lon M. *Enochian Vision Magick: An Introduction and Practical Guide to the Mag-*

ick of Dr. John Dee and Edward Kelley. York
Beach, ME: Weiser Books, 2008.

French, Peter. *John Dee: The World of an Eliz-
abethan Magus.* New York: Dorset Press,
1972.

James, Geoffrey. *The Enochian Evocation of
Dr. John Dee.* York Beach, ME: Weiser
Books, 2009. Rpt. of *The Enochian Magick
of Dr. John Dee: The Most Powerful System
of Magick in its Original, Unexpurgated Form.*
St. Paul, MN: Llewellyn Publishing, 2002.

Laycock, Donald C. *The Complete Enochian Dic-
tionary.* York Beach, ME: Samuel Weiser,
1994.

Leitch, Aaron. *The Angelic Language, Vol. I:
The Complete History and Mythos of the Ton-
gue of the Angels.* Woodbury, MN: Llewellyn
Worldwide, 2010.

—. *The Angelic Language, Vol. II: An Ency-
clopedic Lexicon of the Tongue of the Angels.*
Woodbury, MN: Llewellyn Worldwide, 2010.

Skinner, Stephen, and David Rankine. *Practical
Angel Magic of Dr. John Dee's Enochian
Tables.* Singapore: Golden Hoard Press, 2004.

Szőnyi, György E. *John Dee's Occultism: Magical Exaltation Through Powerful Signs.* Albany, NY: SUNY Press, 2004.

Tyson, Donald. *The Power of the Word: The
Secret Code of Creation.* St. Paul, MN:

Llewellyn Worldwide, 2004. Rpt. of *Tetra-grammaton.* 1998.

Woolley, Benjamin. *The Queen's Conjurer.* New York: Henry Holt & Co., 2001.

Yechidah, Frater. *Enochian Magic in Practice.* Dublin, Ireland: Kerubim Press, 2016.

—. *Enochian Magic in Theory.* Dublin, Ireland: Kerubim Press, 2012.

Zalewski, Pat. *Golden Dawn Enochian Magic.* St. Paul, MN: Llewellyn Publications, 1994.

Book-length publications by Mark Stavish

Sea of Sapphire – Visionary Techniques and Talismanic Magic with the Tree of Life
(IHS Study Guides Vol. 5 – forthcoming)

∼ ∼ ∼

Words of My Teachers – A Study Guide to the IHS Audio Program Series
(IHS Study Guides Vol. 4 – forthcoming)

∼ ∼ ∼

Child of the Sun – Psychic & Physical Rejuvenation in Alchemy and Qabala
(IHS Study Guides Vol. 3)

∼ ∼ ∼

The Inner Way – The Power of Prayer and Belief in Spiritual Practice
(IHS Study Guides Vol. 2)

∼ ∼ ∼

Light on the Path – A Study Guide for Qabala, Alchemy & Astrology
(IHS Study Guides Vol. 1)

∼ ∼ ∼

The Path of Alchemy – Energetic Healing and the World of Natural Magic
(Available in Polish and Russian)

∼ ∼ ∼

Kabbalah for Health and Wellness
(Available in Portuguese and Russian)

(Continued on the following page...)

Freemasonry – Rituals, Symbols and History of the Secret Society
(Available in French, Portuguese, and Spanish)

~ ~ ~

Between the Gates – Lucid Dreaming, Astral Projection and the Body of Light in Western Esotericism
(Available in Portuguese and Russian)

WITH CONTRIBUTIONS BY MARK STAVISH

Howlings from the Pit – A Practical Handbook of Medieval Magic, Goetia & Theurgy
by Dr. Joseph C. Lisiewski, Edited with Commentary by Mark Stavish (2011)

~ ~ ~

The Key to Solomon's Key – Is This the Lost Symbol of Masonry? By Lon Milo DuQuette,
with Introduction by James Wasserman, and Afterword by Mark Stavish (2010)

~ ~ ~

Israel Regardie and the Philosopher's Stone – The Alchemical Arts Brought Down to Earth by Dr. Joseph C. Lisiewski,
Introduction by Mark Stavish (2009)

~ ~ ~

The Red Church, or The Art of Pennsylvania German Braucherei by C.R. Bilardi, Introduction by Mark Stavish (2009)

Support from the Institute for Hermetic Studies

The Institute for Hermetic Studies offers a range of ongoing support to individual students and groups through online materials, seminars, and private tutorial. These include but are not limited to: basic, intermediate, and advanced instruction in the Hermetic Arts and Sciences, astrological consultations, assistance with psychic and spiritual crises, and training for ordination in the Minor and Major Orders of the Church of St. Cyprian the Mage of Antioch. All information regarding our programs is announced in our free electronic newsletter VOXHERMES. For more information contact:

The Institute for Hermetic Studies
P.O. Box 4513
Wyoming, PA 18644-04513

www.hermeticinstitute.org
info@hermeticinstitute.org

Mark Stavish (Pennsylvania) is a respected authority in the study and practice of Western spiritual traditions. He is the author of several books, most recently the first two volumes of IHS Study Guides, *Light on the Path*, *The Inner Way*, and *Child of the Sun*, as well as *The Path of Alchemy*, *Kabbalah for Health and Wellness*, and *Between the Gates – Lucid Dreaming, Astral Projection, and the Body of Light in Western Esotericism*, and has been translated into over nine languages worldwide. He is the founder of both the Institute for Hermetic Studies (Wyoming, Pennsylvania), where he is Director of Studies, and the Louis Claude de St. Martin Fund, a non-profit fund dedicated to the study and practice of esotericism.

Alfred DeStefano III (Oklahoma) teaches mathematics at the university level. In addition to being a "Renaissance Man" of many varied and unique talents, he has assisted in the production of numerous esoteric publications, including the previous volumes of IHS Study Guides and the 7th Edition of Israel Regardie's *The Golden Dawn*, edited by John Michael Greer (Llewellyn).

John Kadai (Toronto) is an ordained priest in the Church of St. Cyprian the Mage of Antioch and holds the Martinist Third Degree. Kadai has worked extensively in the motion picture industry and is an architectural designer. He created the illustration of the angelic talisman that is displayed at the front of this monograph.

Printed in Great Britain
by Amazon